planet earth

ANIMALS AND THEIR

By Tracey West

SCHOLASTIC INC.

New York   Toronto   London   Auckland   Sydney
Mexico City   New Delhi   Hong Kong   Buenos Aires

Contents

Kill or Be Killed

That might sound harsh, but that's the reality for animals in the wild. The natural world is divided into predators and *prey.*

Predators hunt and kill other animals for food. They are equipped with the tools they need to take down animals and tear through flesh—tools like sharp claws, daggerlike teeth, powerful muscles, and hard beaks.

Prey are animals that are hunted, killed, and eaten by other animals. Prey are equipped with tools, too. Some species of prey are fast, so they can outrun or outfly their hunters. Others use camouflage to blend in with their environment, so predators won't spot them. And some kinds of prey use poison or bad smells to keep predators away.

Sometimes, an animal can be both predator *and prey.* **Sound confusing? It's all about the** food chain.

Life in the Chain

A food chain shows who eats what in a particular habitat. For example: grass is eaten by a rabbit, which is eaten by a great horned owl. The arrows between each item in the chain always point in the direction of energy flow—in other words, from the food to the feeder.

All food chains are short. A lot of energy is lost at each step, and after three steps most of the available energy has been expended. This explains why the organisms at the top of food chains (like owls) are very small in number compared with those lower down (like grass plants). After two steps there is simply not enough available energy to support more than a few top predators.

In this book, you'll read about different kinds of animals and their prey. Each one has its own place on the food chain, and each uses strategy to eat, live, and thrive in its environment.

The animals in this book are grouped by *habitat*—the kind of environment they live in. The habitat includes *things like* plant life, animal life, water sources, temperature, and altitude.

The Landscapes of Planet Earth

For each animal, you'll see a picture of its habitat. The animals live in one of the following landscapes:

Mountain Heights

Did you know that mountains cover 24 percent of the Earth's land surface? Mountain-dwelling animals face high altitudes and temperatures that range from severe heat to extreme cold.

Rainforests

Plenty of rain creates a perfect environment for plants to thrive—and provides a rich habitat for all kinds of life.

Open Ocean Depths

Many of the planet's most mysterious creatures live deep in the ocean, beyond where humans can travel.

Great Forests

The trees in the world's forests provide oxygen for the planet, and create a home for a variety of animals from spiders to tigers.

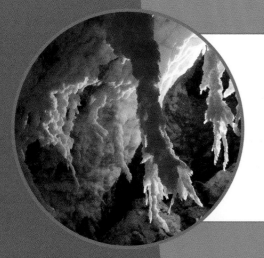

Underworld

How do you live in a cave, deep below the earth, without light? Cave creatures have come up with some amazing ways to survive.

Frozen Poles

The North and South Poles—the Arctic and Antarctic— are two of the world's most extreme environments. Animals that live here must be able to survive subfreezing temperatures.

Great Sands

The blazing hot temperatures of the world's deserts make it difficult for almost any kind of life to survive. The animals that do live there have developed their own strategies to get food and water.

Shallow Seas

These regions of shallow water surround each of the continents. They may form a small part of the world's oceans, but they contain rich areas of life, including coral reefs and forests of seaweed.

Great Plains

Animals thrive on these large, grass-covered plains, which are found on every continent except Antarctica.

Freshwater

Earth is a very watery planet—but only 3 percent of the water is fresh. Humans need fresh water to survive, and we share that water with fish, birds, reptiles, amphibians, and other mammals that live in the world's lakes, rivers, and streams.

PUMA

Puma is an Incan word that means **"powerful."** That's a good name for this *predator* that relies on **strength** and **stealth** to take down its prey.

Anatomy of a Killer

Teeth like knives: A puma has super sharp canine teeth in its lower and upper jaw. When a puma attacks, it sinks these teeth into the prey's flesh. This fierce bite can mean instant death.

Powerful back legs: A puma's long, strong back legs allow it to jump high—as high as six feet! This is useful when chasing prey over rocky mountain terrain.

Sharp claws: Pumas use their claws to climb up trees. A high tree branch is a good place to wait to ambush unsuspecting prey.

Hungry for Humans?

Pumas try to avoid being around humans. That's one reason why they live in mountain areas. However, every year, a number of humans are killed by pumas. The victims are usually people traveling alone at dawn, dusk, or night.

Pumas can be found in deserts, forests, and even swamps!

It's true

A puma will eat another puma if it's hungry enough.

MAMMAL

Species: *Puma concolor*

Also known as: Mountain lion, cougar, panther

Average weight of adult male: 136 pounds

Average length of adult male: 4 feet, not including the 2.5 foot tail

Where it lives: Across North America, as far north as Alaska. Its range extends to western areas of South America, down to Argentina and Chile

Preys on: Deer in North America; and guanaco, a llama-like animal, in South America

Also eats: Rabbits, hares, coyotes, bobcats, porcupines, beavers, opossums, raccoons, and skunks

GRIZZLY BEAR

MAMMAL

Species: *Ursus arctos horribilis*

Also known as: Brown bear

Average weight: Up to 900 pounds

Average length: Up to 8 feet

Where it lives: Alaska and Canada. Fewer than 1,000 live in the western United States.

Preys on: Fish, especially salmon; calves of hoofed mammals, such as elk; small rodents; cutworm moths.

Also eats: Plants such as berries, roots, nuts, grasses and seeds; carrion (dead animals); garbage.

One *grizzly bear* can consume a **ton** of salmon over a **six week** salmon-spawning period. That's **two thousand** pounds!

The Ethiopian wolf is an endangered animal. There are fewer than 400 of them surviving in the wild.

ETHIOPIAN WOLF

This African animal lives in *packs* — but hunts **alone.**

MAMMAL

Species: *Canis simensis*

Also known as: Abyssinian wolf, Simien fox, Simien jackal

Average weight of adult male: Up to 37 pounds

Average length of adult male: 3.1 feet (4 feet, including tail)

Where it lives: Mountain ranges in Ethiopia, on the African continent

Preys on: Small mammals such as grass rats, the giant mole rat, and Starck's hare

Also eats: Baby geese and eggs

The snow leopard's tail is longer than its body, measuring at 4 feet for a large adult. They use their tail for balance and for insulation when lying down.

MAMMAL

Species: *Leo uncia*

Also known as: Ounce, long-haired cat

Average weight of adult male: About 50-90 pounds

Average length of adult male: About 7 feet, including the long tail

Where it lives: The mountains of central Asia; India; and the countries surrounding India in southern Asia. The snow leopard is the highest living land predator in the world; some have been recorded surviving at 19,000 feet.

Preys on: Marmots (small rodents with bushy tails), wild sheep, yak, markhors (large goats with spiraled horns), hares, domestic livestock

Also eats: Some plants

SNOW LEOPARD

These **rarely seen** *cats* have been known to jump **50 feet horizontally** to make a **kill.**

GOLIATH BIRD-EATING TARANTULA

This *fuzzy predator* has some **fierce fangs!**

A chemical in the goliath's venom is used to treat strokes, seizures, and other health problems in humans.

Anatomy of a Killer

Venom injectors: Each of the goliath's fangs is one inch long! When it bites its prey, it injects it with deadly venom. This venom isn't powerful enough to kill humans, but if you were bitten by a goliath, you'd be in serious pain.

Hair attack: If it feels threatened, the goliath shoots out tiny, sharp hairs from its abdomen. The hairs are almost invisible, but they can really irritate human skin.

Noise makers: The goliath can make a noise so loud it can be heard 15 feet away! It makes a hissing sound by rubbing the bristles together on its back legs. The goliath does this to scare away other predators.

A Tasty Treat

Some South Americans like to eat the goliath. They remove the poison sacs and fangs, wrap the spider in a banana leaf, and roast it over a fire.

INSECT

Species: *Theraposa blondi*

Average weight of adult male: 4 ounces

Average size of adult male: 11 inches across, from leg to leg. (Next time you eat dinner, look down at your plate. That's how big the goliath is!)

Where it lives: Rainforests on the coast of northeastern South America

Preys on: Insects, frogs, small snakes, small lizards

Also eats: Larger animals, such as rodents, bats, and baby birds (hence their name)

JAGUAR

It stays *hidden in the shadows* of the rainforest—but its **reputation** as a **top predator** is *no secret.*

MAMMAL

Species: *Panthera onca*

Also known as: El tigre or tigre Americano

Average weight of adult male: 220 to 350 pounds

Average length of adult male: 5.6 to 9 feet, including tail

Where it lives: Mexico and Central and South America

Preys on: Almost anything it can catch. This includes capybaras (a large rodent, related to a guinea pig), peccaries (a piglike wild animal), deer, birds, sloths, armadillos, monkeys, small alligators, turtles, agoutis (a rodent), fish, and mice.

Jaws of Death

A jaguar hunts alone and most often at night, dawn, and dusk. Hunting in dim or dark light allows the jaguar to sneak up on prey without being seen. Then the jaguar pounces—and its powerful jaws get to work.

A jaguar's jaws can pierce the hard shell of a turtle. If the prey is a capybara, the jaguar goes right for the skull. It sinks its canines into a groove in the skull bones, then crushes the skull with one bite. No other big cat is known to have this skull-crushing power.

A jaguar might kill larger prey by pinning it down, then chomping on its neck. The bite paralyzes the animal. Then the jaguar drags it away and chows down.

HARPY EAGLE

This **bird of prey** uses **sharp talons** to grab *meaty mammals* from the rainforest **floor.**

BIRD

Species: *Harpia harpyja*

Average weight: 14 to 20 pounds (females); 8.5 to 12 pounds (males)

Average body length: 35 to 41 inches

Wingspan: Up to 7 feet

Where it lives: Southern Mexico to northern Argentina

Preys on: Macaws, monkeys, sloths, opossums, porcupines, anteaters, young deer, snakes, and iguanas

Patient Predators

Harpy eagles don't soar in the sky like most other eagles. Instead, they save energy by perching in trees for hours, waiting to spot prey. Then they swoop down for the kill.

One army ant can't do much, but **thousands together** can take down **larger prey**.

ARMY ANTS

INSECT

Species: *Eciton burchellii*

Also known as: Legionary ants

Average size of ant colony: 700,000 ants

Where it lives: Eciton burchellii live in South America, but other species of army ants can be found all over the world.

Preys on: Other ants, spiders, and scorpions

On the March

Every morning thousands of army ants march out of the colony in columns like soldiers. When they find prey, they swarm it, inject it with venom, and tear it to pieces. Then they share the food.

SHORTFIN MAKO SHARK

It takes a **fast shark** like this one to *prey* on **fast fish**.

Anatomy of a Killer

Torpedo shape: The long, sleek body is perfect for slicing through water.

Maximum thrust: The shape of the tail helps propel the shark through the water.

Sharp teeth: These help the shark cut up larger prey.

Sword Fight

Swordfish are one of the mako shark's main prey. But swordfish have been known to put up a fight using their long, sharp bills to defend themselves from predators. There are reports that captured makos have been scarred from swordfish fights.

A Need for Speed

The mako might be the fastest fish in the ocean. Mako sharks have been clocked swimming up to 35 mph over distances. Other reports have them zipping along from 60–80 mph in short bursts.

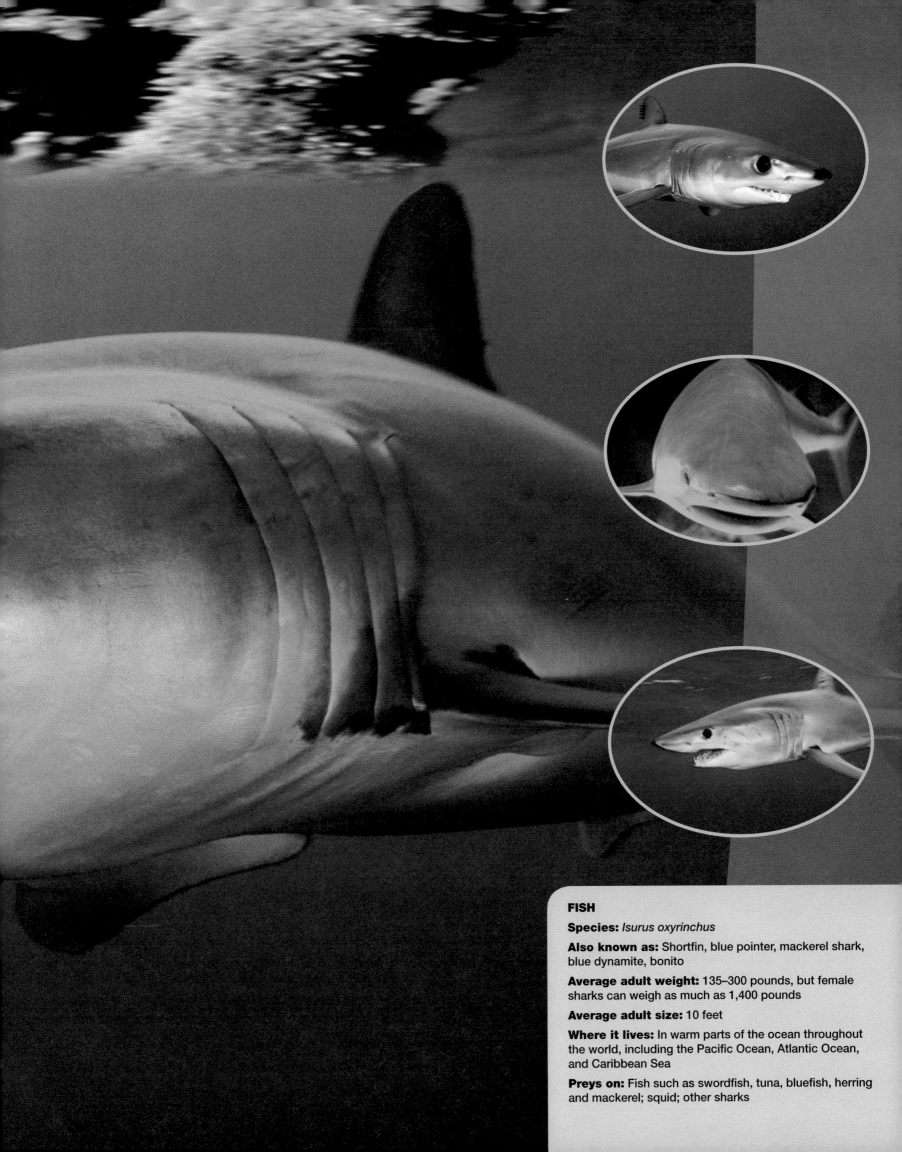

FISH

Species: *Isurus oxyrinchus*

Also known as: Shortfin, blue pointer, mackerel shark, blue dynamite, bonito

Average adult weight: 135–300 pounds, but female sharks can weigh as much as 1,400 pounds

Average adult size: 10 feet

Where it lives: In warm parts of the ocean throughout the world, including the Pacific Ocean, Atlantic Ocean, and Caribbean Sea

Preys on: Fish such as swordfish, tuna, bluefish, herring and mackerel; squid; other sharks

BOX JELLYFISH

Deadly venom gives this creature *super stinging power.*

Stinging Cells

As many as 15 tentacles dangle from the body of the box jellyfish. Each tentacle is covered with up to 5,000 cells that release a powerful venom when they come in contact with prey. Ouch!

FISH

Species: *Chironex fleckeri*

Also known as: Sea wasp, marine stinger

Average weight: Up to 4.4 pounds

Average length: 10 feet

Where it lives: The Indian and southern Pacific Oceans, especially in the waters around northern Australia

Preys on: Small fish and crustaceans such as shrimp

Built-in Bait

What's that glowing on the dark ocean floor? A curious fish swims closer to find out, when . . . gulp! An anglerfish swallows it up. Only the female anglerfish has this "fishing rod." It's actually a piece of spine that hangs above the fish's mouth. Tiny bacteria make the lure glow.

DEEP-SEA ANGLERFISH

This fish uses a **glowing** "fishing rod" to lure *prey.*

FISH

Species: *Lophius piscatorius*

Also known as: Monkfish, black devilfish, triple-wart sea devil

Length: From just a few inches long, to as long as 4 feet

Where it lives: In the Atlantic and Antarctic Oceans

Preys on: Fish, worms, crustaceans

The sperm whale is the only animal with a throat wide enough to swallow a human being whole!

A Huge Head

The sperm whale's giant head makes up one-third of its body length. Inside this enormous cranium is the biggest brain of any mammal on Earth.

MAMMAL

Species: *Physeter macrocephalus*

Also known as: Cachalot

Average weight of adult male: 43.6 tons

Average length of adult male: 53 feet

Where it lives: Most of the world's oceans, in deep waters, except for the icy waters near the poles

Preys on: Fish, including sharks, and squid

A Mammoth Mystery

This massive mammal eats about 1,000 pounds of food a day. So how does the whale catch enough to eat?

Scientists have some guesses. The lower jaw of a sperm whale is white, and squid might be attracted to it.

Another guess has to do with sound. Sperm whales communicate by making loud clicks. The sonic waves might stun squid, leaving them helpless while the whale gulps them down.

SPERM WHALE

These deep-sea divers eat *1,000 pounds* of fish and squid **every day!**

WOLVERINE

Known as a **"glutton,"** the wolverine eats just about *anything* it can dig its **claws** into.

A wolverine is largely nocturnal and during its waking hours will cover as much as 45 miles a day in search of food.

Anatomy of a Killer

Broad feet: The shape of its partly webbed feet allows the wolverine to walk on snow without sinking. Hairs on the soles of its feet provide grip when the wolverine walks on ice.

The nose knows: A wolverine relies on its super sense of smell to track down prey.

Sharp claws: A wolverine can use its claws to scoop fish out of the water.

Meat slicers: With its large teeth and strong jaw muscles, the wolverine can tear through skin, meat, and bone.

Small but Powerful

An adult reindeer weighs around 400 pounds. So how does a 50 pound wolverine take it down? It uses strength—and strategy. The wolverine finds a trail in the forest that it knows is used by reindeer. Then it climbs up a tree and waits. When a reindeer passes by, the wolverine lunges. It digs its claws into the reindeer's back—and won't let go. The weight of the wolverine drags down the reindeer. Then it finishes the job with its strong jaws.

MAMMAL

Species: *Gulo gulo*

Also known as: Glutton, carcajou, skunk bear, devil bear

Average weight: 20-66 pounds

Average size: 26-36 inches long (not including the tail, which is 5-10 inches long)

Where it lives: In northern Europe and through northern North America

Preys on: Mammals such as deer, moose, wild sheep, elk, rabbits, beavers, squirrels, reindeer, arctic hares, arctic wolves, arctic lemmings; land birds such as grouse and snow geese; fish

Also eats: Roots, berries, eggs, insect grubs, carrion

SIBERIAN TIGER

These *big cats* use the cover of the forest to stalk their prey.

MAMMAL

Species: *Panthera tigris alaica*

Also known as: Amur tiger

Average weight: 397–660 pounds

Average length: Up to 10 feet, including the tail

Where it lives: In eastern Russia, and in some parts of China and North Korea

Preys on: Large mammals such as elk, red deer, wild boar

Solitary Stalkers

Like other kinds of tigers, Siberian tigers prefer to hunt alone—often waiting until sunset before setting out. Although their bodies are large, they are able to walk silently in the darkness. They look and listen for any sign of prey. When it spots prey, the tiger crouches down. It slowly creeps toward the prey from behind or from the side. When it is close enough—at least 85 feet away—it springs from its hiding place and pounces. Then the tiger delivers a bite to the back of the neck. This severs the spinal cord and usually causes instant death.

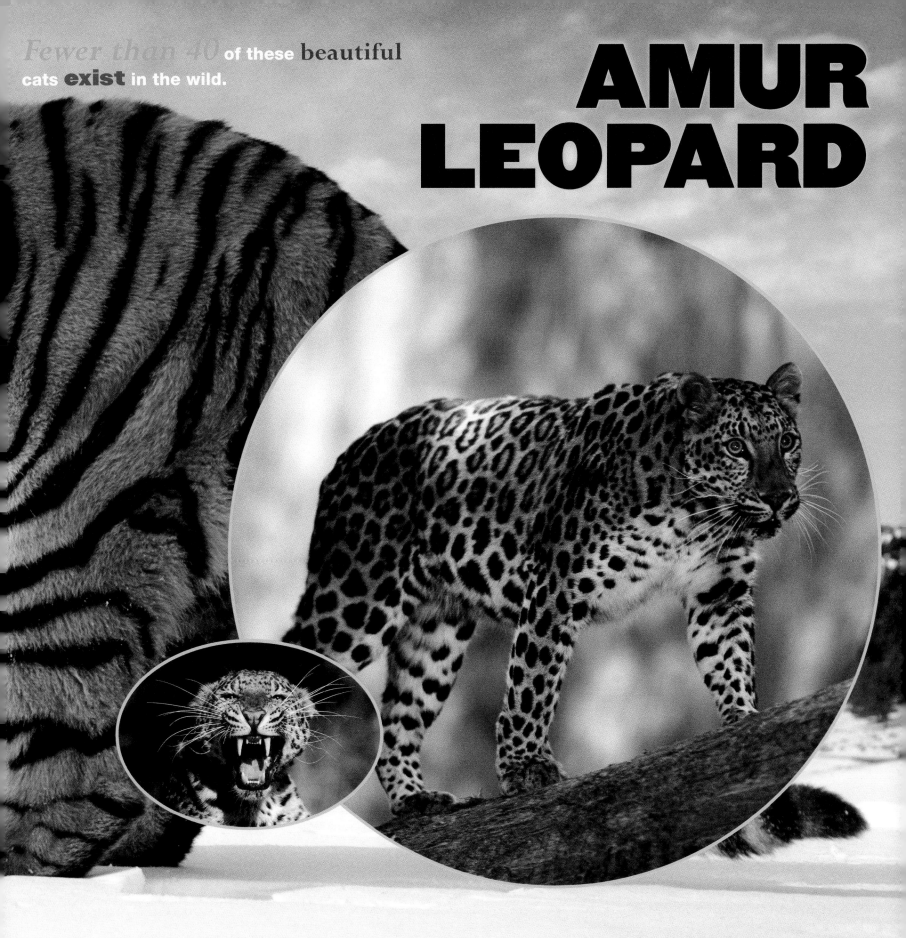

AMUR LEOPARD

Night Hunter

Like other leopards, the Amur leopard hunts alone, at night, and carries its food into the branches of a tree to eat. An Amur leopard has longer fur than other leopards. This keeps it warm in the cold.

MAMMAL

Species: *Panthera pardus orientalis*

Also known as: Far East leopard, Manchurian leopard, Korean leopard

Length: Up to 4 feet

Where it lives: A very small area on the border of Russia, China, and North Korea

Preys on: Roe deer, sika deer, hares, badgers

MEXICAN FREE-TAILED BAT

Mexican free-tailed bats have been recorded at speeds of 60 mph!

One colony of these **fast flyers** can eat *millions of insects* **each** night.

Insect Eaters

Mexican free-tailed bats use their amazing flying abilities to catch insects. These bats fly really high—at altitudes of more than 10,000 feet—higher than any other bat! Flying this high gives them a clear flight path, so they're not blocked by trees or other tall structures. When they're up this high, the bats get an added bonus: They sometimes encounter large groups of insects and feast while they fly.

Inside a Bat Colony

Mexican free-tailed bats form the largest colonies of any warm-blooded animal on Earth. In Bracken Cave, Texas, 20 million bats eat roughly 200 tons of insects every night. A single brown bat can catch 1,200 mosquito-sized insects

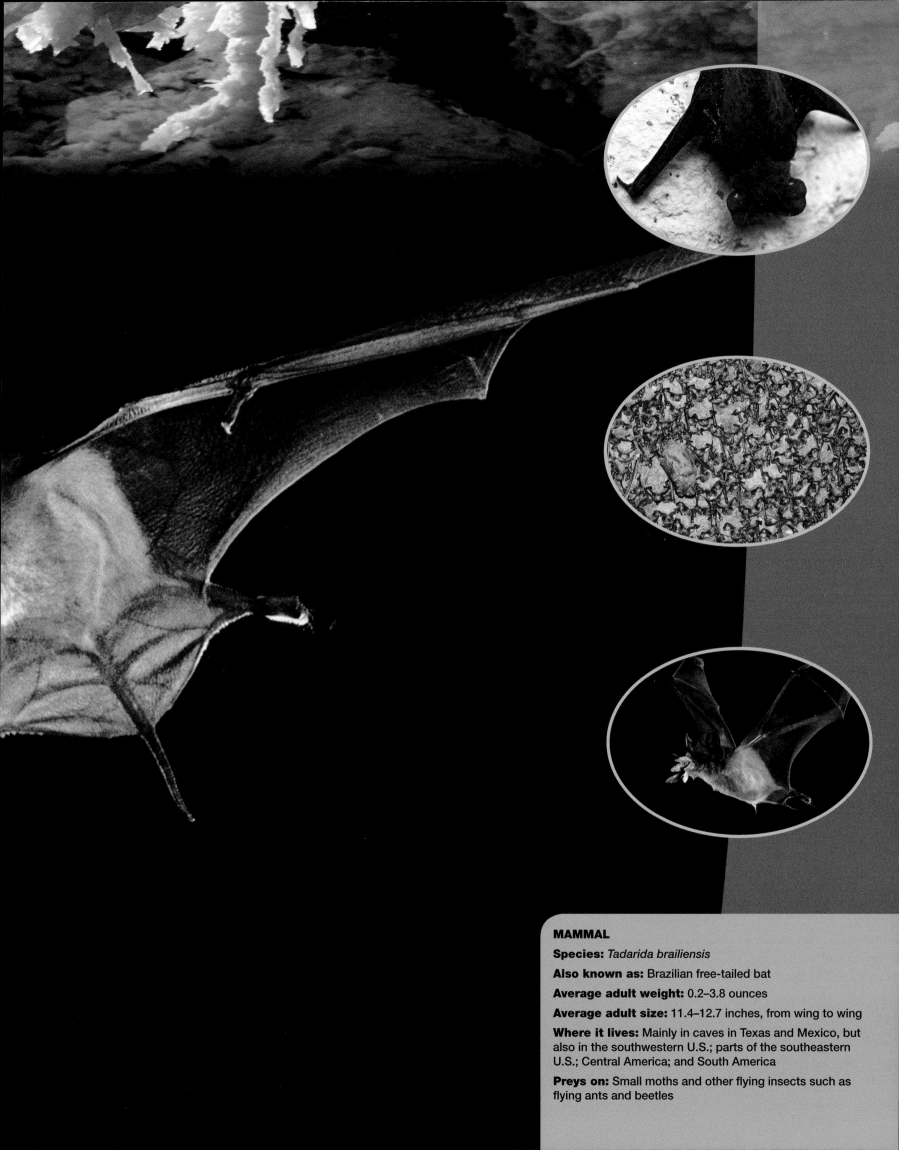

MAMMAL

Species: *Tadarida brailiensis*

Also known as: Brazilian free-tailed bat

Average adult weight: 0.2–3.8 ounces

Average adult size: 11.4–12.7 inches, from wing to wing

Where it lives: Mainly in caves in Texas and Mexico, but also in the southwestern U.S.; parts of the southeastern U.S.; Central America; and South America

Preys on: Small moths and other flying insects such as flying ants and beetles

GREEN TREE FROG

Fly-By Food

Most of Australia's green tree frogs live in rainforest areas, munching on insects. But some frogs have a special diet. At twilight 110,000 little bent-wing bats erupt from Bat Cleft, a limestone cave in Queensland, Australia. The green tree frog can be found perching on rocks at the entrance. When young bats fly out of the cave, the tree frogs gobble them up!

AMPHIBIAN

Species: *Litoria caerulea*

Also known as: White's Tree Frog

Average length: 4 inches

Where it lives: Northwestern, northern, eastern, and southeastern areas of Australia

Preys on: Insects, birds and rodents

Also eats: Little bent-winged bats

This **predator** **can go** without food for *6 years* **if it has to!**

No Eyes, No Problem

This unusual creature has eyes under its skin, but they don't work. Who needs to see when you live in the dark? If prey is near, the salamander's skin detects the prey's movements.

TEXAS BLIND CAVE SALAMANDER

AMPHIBIAN

Species: *Typhlomolge rathbuni*

Average Length: 3 ¼– 5 ⅜ inches

Where it lives: In caves in the San Marcos, Texas area

Preys on: Shrimp, snails, and amphipods (small crustaceans that live in water)

Glow-in-the-Dark Mucus

The cave glowworm is the larva of a small gnat. After the larva hatches from an egg, it spins a silk strand from its mouth. This strand dangles down from the cave ceiling. The glowworm adds balls of mucus to the strand, making it look like a string of pearls.

At night, the glowworms go to work. They hang out inside a mucus tube at the top of the line. Then their tails begin to glow. This illuminates the mucus balls on the line, making them look like lights at a party.

But this trap is no party for passing insects! Attracted by the light, they get stuck in the sticky strands. The glowworm reels in the line like a fishing pole. Then it feeds on the still-living prey. Way to glow!

INSECT

Species: *Arachnocampa luminosa*

Average size of adult larvae: 1.2–1.6 inches

Average length of silk strand: 2–9 inches

Where it lives: In caves, tunnels, and other places in New Zealand. Other types of cave glowworms live in Australia.

Preys on: Insects such as midges, flies, cockroaches, and beetles

These larvae trap prey with *strings of silk* that look like glowing beads.

CAVE GLOWWORMS

POLAR BEAR

These **strong**, patient predators are at the top of the food chain in the frozen north. They're also the *largest* land-dwelling **carnivores**.

Anatomy of a Killer

Powerful muscles: The polar bear is so strong it can pull a 1,000 pound whale out of the water.

The nose knows: The polar bear's nose sniffs out prey hiding under snow and ice.

Killer claws: Short, curved claws are good for ripping through ice to get to prey.

Webbed paws: A polar bear can use its webbed paws to speed through the sea as fast as four miles per hour.

Ferocious bite: Small prey, such as a young seal, is helpless in the jaws of a polar bear.

Clear fur, dark skin: Polar bear fur looks white, but it's actually see-through. Sun shines through the fur and gets absorbed by the bear's dark skin. The fur takes on the color of whatever's around it. Polar bears are usually around snow and ice, so their fur looks white.

Two Big Bears

The polar bear and brown Grizzly bear are the largest meat-eating animals that live on land.

MAMMAL

Species: *Ursus maritimus*

Also known as: White Bear, Ice Bear, Sea Bear, Nanuk

Average weight of adult male: 900–1,600 pounds

Average size of adult male: Up to 7–8 feet long, not including the 3–5 inch tail

Where it lives: Throughout the Arctic region

Preys on: Seals, including ringed seals, bearded seals, and harp seals; walruses; narwhals, beluga whales; and sea ducks

Also eats: Plants such as seaweed, algae, and grass

KILLER WHALE

Many of a killer whale's **teeth** are *4 inches long!*

The killer whale is the largest member of the dolphin family.

MAMMAL

Species: *Orcinus orca*

Also known as: Orca

Average weight of adult male: 5 tons

Average length of adult male: 26 feet

Where it lives: In oceans all over the world from the polar regions to the equator

Preys on: Fish such as tuna and salmon; seals, squid, sea lions, sea turtles, porpoises, dolphins, and whales

Pod Predators

Killer whales live in small groups called pods. There are usually between 5–40 whales in a pod. Pods work together to catch food. Here are two pod-hunting strategies:

1. Ganging up: A pod of killer whales encircling their prey, such as a school of fish, forcing them together into one area.

Then they take turns feeding.

2. Push play: Some whales slide out of the water onto the shore, where seals or penguins gather. The scared seals and penguins jump into the water to get away—right into the waiting mouths of other whales in the pod!

LEOPARD SEAL

Leopard seals are named for their spotted coats, but they live up to their name and are **fearsome** hunters.

Anatomy of a Killer

Long, sharp teeth: Perfect for tearing apart prey.

Large foreflippers: These make seals speedy swimmers.

Built-in filtration: Special lobes on their jaws filter krill from the water.

MAMMAL

Species: *Hydrurga leptonyx*

Weight: Up to 840 pounds

Average length: 10–11.5 feet

Where it lives: In waters around Antarctica and sub-Antarctic areas, such as Australia and South America

Preys on: Krill (tiny, shrimp-like creatures), penguins, fish, squid, crabeater seals, and fur seals

ARCTIC FOX

The *fur* of this fox can keep it **warm** when the temperature plummets to -94 degrees Fahrenheit!

A Camouflage Coat

In the summer, the Arctic fox's coat is brown or gray, helping it to blend into rocks and plants. In winter, the coat turns white (or blue-gray, in Iceland) so that the fox blends in with the snow. This camouflage helps the fox hunt prey without being seen.

MAMMAL

Species: *Alopex lagopus*

Also known as: Polar fox

Average weight of adult male: 8.3 pounds

Average length of adult male: 22 inches, not including the 12-inch long tail

Where it lives: Coastal regions of Arctic lands, including far northern North America, Greenland, Iceland, Europe, and Asia

Preys on: Lemmings, voles, squirrels, birds, and fish

Also eats: Some berries and vegetables; bird eggs; dead birds, fish, and seals

GREAT HORNED OWL

The horned owl is named for the tufts of feathers on its head, which look like two horns.

Anatomy of a Killer

The great horned owl prefers to hunt at sunrise and sundown. To catch its favorite prey, rabbits, the owl perches high atop a tree limb or pole. When it spots prey, it dives sharply down to the ground. The sound of flapping wings would scare a rabbit away. Luckily for the owl, it has soft feathers on the edges of its wings. This allows the owl to swoop down in almost complete silence. It quickly grabs the surprised rabbit in its talons and flies off.

Talons of Terror

This owl's talons are sharp and strong enough to capture and kill prey instantly.

The *great horned owl* is one of the only animals that will **eat skunks.**

BIRD

Species: *Bubo virginianus*

Average weight: 32.12–88.25 ounces

Average length: 18–25 inches

Average wingspan: 36–60 inches

Where it lives: From Arctic regions of North America down to eastern South America

Preys on: Mainly small mammals such as rabbits, squirrels, mice, raccoons, and moles; birds such as geese and herons; reptiles such as snakes and lizards; amphibians such as frogs and salamanders; fish; and some insects

Also eats: Roadkill

The Hidden Watcher

When this snake hunts, it buries its body under the sand. Only the tip of its tail and top of its head stick out. It waits, hidden, until a lizard passes by. Then the snake grips the lizard in its mouth, poisons it with venom, and swallows it down.

A sidewinding snake moves forward by keeping its body sideways.

PERINGUEY'S SIDEWINDING ADDER

This tiny, *poisonous* snake hides in desert sands to ambush its prey.

REPTILE

Species: *Bitis peringueyi*

Also known as:
Peringuey's viper, the sidewinding adder

Average length: 8–10 inches

Where it lives:
The Namib Desert in southwestern Africa

Preys on: Lizards

How to Hunt for Gerbils

Here's how a fennec fox hunts for one of its favorite foods: gerbils.

1. The fennec fox keeps cool in a hollow during the heat of the day.

2. While the sun is setting, the fox ventures out. It uses its excellent night vision to spot prey as it races across the sand. The fennec fox has fur on its feet, which helps it to grip the loose sand.

3. The fennec fox's large ears help it to listen for prey. The fox pinpoints where the sound is coming from and then silently stalks its prey.

4. Finally, the fox pins the gerbil to the ground with its paw before sinking its teeth in. Yum!

MAMMAL

Species: *Fennecus zerda*

Average weight: 3.3 pounds

Average length: 14–16 inches, not including a 7 to 12.2 inch tail

Where it lives: In the Sahara desert in North Africa, and the Sinai and Arabian peninsulas

Preys on: Rodents such as gerbils, reptiles, and insects

Also eats: Plants and eggs

FENNEC FOX

The world's *smallest fox* pounces on **prey** in the desert.

Although fennec foxes are the smallest canines in the world, their ears are 6 inches long! That's over one-third of this fox's full body length!

CALIFORNIA SEA LION

How deep can a sea lion dive? The deepest dive recorded was 900 feet.

Deep-Sea Divers

The food a sea lion loves to eat lives deep beneath the waves, so a sea lion spends about 15 hours a day diving in search of food.

Anatomy of a Killer

Whiskers help out: The sea lion's whiskers feel out food on the ocean floor.

Sleek form: The shape of a sea lion's body is ideal for diving deep underwater.

Hold your breath: A sea lion's nostrils close up when it dives. This lets the sea lion stay underwater for up to 40 minutes.

Move it: Front flippers propel the sea lion through the water

Power steering: The hind flippers steer the sea lion

Crushing power: A sea lion doesn't chew its food, but its back molars are great for crushing hard crab shells.

These sleek swimmers dive daily in search of *tasty fish* and **squid**.

MAMMAL

Species: *Zalophus californianus*

Average weight of adult male: 800 pounds

Average length of adult male: 7 feet

Where it lives: From Canada down to the California coast and parts of Mexico; the Galápagos Islands

Preys on: squid, octopus; fish such as hake, northern anchovy, opaleye, herring, rockfish, mackerel; crustaceans such as crabs; clams; and small sharks

RED LIONFISH

This *pretty fish* packs some [...] and a *strategy* that's perfect for *hunting* in coral reefs.

FISH

Species: *Pterois volitans*

Also known as: Turkey fish, fire-fish

Average length: 1 foot

Where it lives: Coral reefs and rocky coasts of the Indian and southern Pacific Oceans

Preys on: Small fish and shrimp

Fancy Fins

With its colorful, striped body, and frilly fins, this fish might not look like a top predator to you. But in the coral reef, the lionfish is at the top of the food chain—and those fins are the reason: The lionfish uses the fins on the sides of its body like fans to push smaller fish into confined spaces in the coral reef. Then it gobbles them down! There are more fins on the back of the lionfish—as many as 18 fins that are shaped like sharp spikes. Scientists think these fins keep the lionfish from becoming prey to larger sea creatures. Those spikes pack a painful sting!

SEA KRAIT

Land and Sea

Most sea snakes spend their whole lives in the sea. But sea kraits will lay their eggs on land. Large scales on the snake's belly help them move over ground and climb up trees.

The venom of a banded sea krait is 10 times more poisonous than the venom of a rattlesnake!

REPTILE

Species: *Laticauda colubrina*

Also known as: Banded sea krait

Maximum length: Adult females can reach 50 inches long

Where it lives: Waters around the coast of New Guinea, the Philippines, Sri Lanka, southeast Asia, Japan, and the Pacific Islands

Preys on: Eels and small fish

Do you like **anchovies** on your pizza? This shark likes to *eat them fresh.*

Super Snout

Sharp eyesight and an excellent sense of smell help the blue shark track down prey. The sensitive snout helps the shark zero in on a prey's location.

FISH

Species: *Prioncae glauca*

Also known as: Great blue shark, blue dog, blue whaler

Average weight: About 300–400 pounds

Maximum length: About 12 feet

Where it lives: In temperate and tropical ocean waters all over the world

Preys on: Small fish, such as anchovies; squid; some crabs and shrimp; birds; other sharks

BLUE SHARK

LION

Anatomy of a Killer

Powerful legs: A lion can run as fast as 40 miles an hour and jump as far as 40 feet in a single bound!

Curved claws: A lion uses its strong, curved claws to grip prey and tackle it to the ground. They are sharp enough to pierce animal hide.

Excellent ears: If prey is nearby, a lion will hear it.

Jaws of death: Strong jaw muscles allow a lion to crush the windpipe of a zebra or other prey, suffocating it. Long teeth as sharp as knives can deliver a fatal bite to smaller prey.

Night vision: A lion's eyes have a special reflective layer that allow them to see in dim light.

Hunting in a Pride

Lions live in small groups called prides. A pride can have just a few lions, or as many as 40. A pride of lions will work together to hunt prey.

Females, who are smaller and faster than males, do most of the hunting. They use strategy to hunt: The fastest ones will chase the prey while the stronger ones take down the prey.

MAMMAL

Species: *Panthera leo*

Average weight of adult male: 330–530 pounds

Average adult size of adult male: Between 6–7 feet, not including the 3.3-foot long tail

Where it lives: In parts of Africa and the Fir Forest of India

Preys on: Wildebeests, zebras, baby elephants, baby rhinos, rodents, reptiles, insects, and crocodiles

Also eats: Food stolen from other big cats, wild dogs, or hyenas

TIBETAN FOX

Two Is Better Than One

When a male Tibetan fox and female fox decide to mate, they usually stay together for life. They hunt together, too, looking for their favorite prey: the black lipped pika. The foxes share whatever food they catch.

MAMMAL

Species: *Vulpis ferrilata*

Also known as: Sand fox

Average weight: Up to 8.8 pounds

Average length: Up to 2 feet, not including the 1.5-foot long tail

Where it lives: Tibet, and areas of China, India, and Nepal

Preys on: Black lipped pikas, rodents, hares, rabbits, small ground birds—and just about anything else they can catch.

Small animals on the Asian plains are **easy prey** for this predator.

Amazing Eaters

Strong teeth and a super digestive system mean the hyena can eat just about anything. Almost nothing gets wasted when a hyena chows down. It will eat the bones and even teeth of an animal—almost everything except the hair and horns.

MAMMAL

Species: *Crocuta crocuta*

Also known as: Laughing hyena

Maximum weight: 180 pounds

Maximum length: 6.6 feet

Where it lives: In Africa, south of the Sahara Desert

Preys on: Wildebeest, gazelles, zebras, young hippos, fish

SPOTTED HYENA

Unlike other hyenas, the *spotted hyena* aggressively **hunts down** prey.

MAMMAL

Species: *Canis lupus arctos*

Also known as: White wolf, polar wolf

Average weight of adult male: Up to 100 pounds

Average length: Up to 5 feet, not including a 13–23 inch tail

Where it lives: Far northern regions of North America, and parts of Greenland

Preys on: Caribou, musk-oxen, hares, lemmings

Pack Hunters

Arctic wolves hunt in packs and use strength to bring down larger animals. Although they are not super fast runners, they have stamina and can keep going for long distances until their prey tires out.

ARCTIC WOLF

As white as *arctic snow,* this wolf takes down large prey using **strength and teamwork.**

NILE CROCODILE

Nile crocodiles **are reported to kill** up to *200 humans* **each year.**

Making a Comeback

In the 1960s, hunting almost caused Nile crocodiles to become extinct. Laws protecting the crocs have helped their species make a comeback.

Fishing Party

Crocodiles usually hunt alone. But when fish migrate, crocs sometimes team up. Several crocs will block off an area of the water, trapping the fish. Then it's time for a feeding frenzy!

Nile crocodiles have been seen to "fish" with their tails, too. They wave their tails, pushing the fish toward the riverbank. Then they snap up the trapped fish in their jaws.

Good Moms

Nile crocodiles are the best reptile parents on earth. They closely guard their eggs until they hatch. Then they gently scoop up the baby crocs into their mouth and carry the newborns to the water. The babies get protection from Mom for a whole year before they go off on their own.

REPTILE

Species: *Crocodylus niloticus*

Average weight: 500 pounds

Average length: 16 feet

Where it lives: In Africa, south of the Sahara desert; and parts of Madagascar

Preys on: Fish, zebras, small hippos, porcupines, wildebeest, birds, other crocodiles

Also eats: Carrion

Mini Monsters?

When you hear "piranha," you probably think of ferocious schools of fish that tear apart their prey with their sharp teeth. It is possible that humans have been attacked by piranhas; however the truth is much less scary. . . . Piranhas do have strong jaws and sharp teeth. But mainly they use them to tear apart prey that is about their size, or smaller.

There are 20 different species of piranha. The red-bellied piranha has the sharpest teeth of them all.

These fish **tear apart prey** with their sharp teeth. But do they prey on *humans*, too?

RED-BELLIED PIRANHA

FISH

Species: *Serrasalmus nattereri*

Maximum weight: 8 pounds

Maximum length: 1–2 feet

Where it lives: In South America from northern Argentina to Colombia, especially in the Amazon River

Preys on: Other fish

Also eats: Stories say that if a large animal is injured and falls into the water, the piranha will swarm around it in a feeding frenzy.

JAPANESE GIANT SALAMANDER

The **giant salamander** is the world's *largest amphibian.* It can live to be 80 years old.

Suction Power

The giant salamander has poor eyesight. To find prey, it uses sensory organs on its body and head. When it finds prey, it quickly opens and closes its mouth. Suction pulls the prey inside.

AMPHIBIAN

Species: *Andrias japonicus*

Average weight: 55 pounds

Average length: 6.5 feet

Where it lives: In Japan, northern Kyushu Island and western Honshu

Preys on: Fish, mice, insects, and crustaceans such as crabs

Death Squeeze

When the anaconda takes down larger prey, such as a deer, it uses its whole body. It will wait in the water until the deer comes to drink. Then it will grab the prey by the neck, wrap its body around it, and squeeze. This powerful hug suffocates the deer. Then the anaconda drags it into the water and swallows it whole.

This *huge* snake squeezes the life out of its prey.

REPTILE

Species: *Eunectes murinus*

Also known as: Giant anaconda

Average length: 16 feet

Where it lives: Tropical waters east of the Andes Mountains and in Trinidad

Preys on: Caimans; mammals such as capybara, deer, tapirs, and peccaries; turtles; birds

GREEN ANACONDA

PROTECT PLANET EARTH,
It's the Only One We've Got . . .

Here are some ways you can help preserve our extraordinary Planet Earth.

Here's a Bright Idea! If you're leaving a room for more than 30 seconds, flip the switch. You'll save energy—and reduce your energy bill, too!

Buy Recycled. Encourage your parents to buy recycled paper products for your house.

Reusable Containers Rule. When it comes to your lunch, the less packaging, the better. Individually wrapped snacks and drinks waste resources. Instead, use reusable containers from home to bring your food to and from school.

Down the Tubes. Why not turn off the faucet when you're brushing your teeth? You'll save lots of water from going down the drain.

Put Your Computer to Sleep. Using a screensaver on your computer uses more energy than if you let it go to sleep. So change the preferences on your computer and give it a rest.

Bring Your Own Bag. If you're going shopping, bring your own reusable bags with you. Plastic bags are made from petroleum (aka oil) and paper bags are made from trees. So if you bring your own reusable bag, you won't be wasting either!

Recharge Your Batteries. Buy rechargeable batteries that you can reuse, rather than disposable batteries that you throw away.

Remember the Three R's. Reduce. Reuse. Recycle. These are important ways to cut down on consumption and waste.

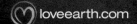